PUPPY TRAINING

"HOW TO HOUSEBREAK YOUR PUPPY IN ONLY 7 DAYS"

ANTHONY PORTOKALOGLOU

Disclaimer Notice

The techniques described in this book are for informational purposes only. All attempts have been made by the author to provide real and accurate content. No responsibility will be taken by the author for any damages cost by misuse of the content described in this book. Please consult a licensed professional before utilizing the information of this book.

Contents

You gazed into those big adorable eyes and that puppy seemed to see right into your soul, looking so lovable and cuddly that you were immediately hooked! It felt like it was love at first sight! That little baby was simply impossible to resist! But now you have that sweet little baby home and you are thinking perhaps you purchased a crocodile instead of a puppy as he wants to bite everything in sight hands, walls, shoes, chairs... everything! The little darling chases every moving object and has no idea of where or when to go potty. Understand that whatever puppies require from us in effort, they give back so much more than they take. Their cute presence elicits our best impulses that are deep within us and their contribution to our lives makes us better, caring people for the benefit of those around us! So, don't despair, as this book will give you the tools to have your puppy trained in record time!

Chapter 1: Understanding Your Puppy and the Pack Mentality

To train your puppy you first need to understand how your puppy assimilates his surroundings and where you will fit in his social structure. In canine's the pack mentality is very real, even when they are raised by humans.

First you must realize that in packs there is always an alpha. To your new puppy, you are simply a bigger dog. Your puppy has the intention of being the alpha, and your puppy will do whatever it wants, in the belief that it is alpha puppy until you show it otherwise. Being the "alpha" is not to you given it must be earned by you. There are dozens of videos on Facebook that are perfect illustrations of how disobedient, destructive and obstinate a pup can be when they have determined that they and not you are the alpha male.

In packs the leader is the alpha, he eats first, walks first, and controls the territory and will fight to maintain his leadership. This attitude is still entrenched in your puppy's DNA and your puppy is very much orientated to the idea it makes its own rules during those early months. Within that lovable diminutive ball of fluff is an unruly wolf pup waiting to defeat the leader and gain dominance of its territory. Pack leaders do not allow youngsters and lower pack members to have what they want when they want it. They use their authority to make them wait, sometimes denying them altogether. This sets a formidable example of who's in charge and teaches forbearance and self-control to high-strung, excitable young dogs. Making your dog sit and ignore things that excite him is a good way to establish your Leadership. It is also unwise to have your puppy sleep in bed with you. The alpha leader only allows his chosen female into his sleeping area. Any pack members failing to observe this strict rule do so at their peril. So, it's hardly unpredicted when owners allow their dogs into their bedroom that the puppies get the wrong idea. It is typical for a dog who occupies the owners sleeping quarters to assume that he is the alpha male and eventually can develop improper behavior. Oftentimes it is disobedience, more often it's possessiveness that can transform into aggression. Dogs are usually clever, maybe not as much as portrayed in television, but there is one area in which they are foolproof and that is reading other animals and that includes you!

Your dog will sense every slight change in your mood and react accordingly. If you are afraid he is going to misbehave he'll do exactly that. Pack Leaders control the pack by mental strength. You must convince him that you are that alpha male.

Your puppy will begin teething around two months of age and will want to bite and chew everything (including you). One technique to minimize this, is when your puppy gets his mouth on your hand quickly push your finger into his mouth until it reaches the gag reflex area. He will quickly lose interest in biting your hand to avoid that gag feeling. Remember to scold your puppy when you find him chewing something you don't want him to. A spank with a newly chewed shoe (item) will help your puppy know that he is not allowed to do that. Point and the chewed item and forcefully say "no". Once this is done, a light spank again will confirm the rebuke. Dogs have thicker skin than humans and the spank is not necessarily to inflict pain, but to show leadership. Remember your goal is to impose your will and become the alpha male. Do not punish your puppy after an incident has passed. They do not process information the same way, or reason the same way we do. To correct your puppy when time has passed in unfair and confusing to your puppy.

Play fighting is a good social skill for your puppy and will produce bonding between you as his master and establish your leadership level. It is important to show the puppy you are stronger than him and therefore the alpha. Holding your puppy down is an effective technique to establish dominance (not too firm and just a few seconds). Rolling the puppy over is another way of establishing your authority. Make sure you have toys for your puppy to play with and use them to play with him. Get a good variety, soft toys and hard toys to chew on, especially while he is teething. Tugging is a fun way to prove you are stronger and promote playfulness.

There are a variety of techniques to ensure that your puppy grows up to be an obedient, social and loving dog. It is also important to try and make sure your puppy associates with other dogs as they grow to help promote a pack mentality and good social skills. Also, in the early stages of your puppy be sure they have opportunity to interact with a variety of people to help them become social and friendly. It is a good idea to have your puppy interact with children as well. Children can be very intimidating to dogs and so for them to acclimate to them is very important. However, the most important thing is to make sure your puppy feels loved, by playing, petting, and treats. Puppies love human contact and affection. They are responsive both to a strong leader, but it is just as important to be a nurturing parent. It is essential to enjoy outdoor activities with your puppy whenever possible. When teaching your pet discipline, take a lesson from alpha wolves. Do not bark! Use the tone of your voice, your posture and uniformity to express your leadership. The wolves who are not an alpha but want to be alpha are the ones who mouth off. They have something to prove. You do not. You are already alpha and it is imperative that you act like one. Consistent treatment of your puppy lets him know what is expected of him. Prompt action against misbehavior shows him that you will not abide disobedience far better than all the yelling in the world. To control your puppy, you must first be in control of yourself! Self-control is the ability to control impulses and reactions, and is another name for self-discipline. Self-control, an aspect of inhibitory control, is the ability to regulate one's emotions, thoughts, and behavior in the face of temptations and impulses. As an executive function, self-control is a cognitive process that is necessary for regulating one's behavior in order to achieve specific goals.If you expect self-discipline from your puppy you must first learn to set the example. There will be many times in training your puppy that you will feel like your self-control is tested to its very limits. You will be tempted to wrongfully punish your pet when your life has been inconvenienced or your favorite things destroyed. Self-control is vital for overcoming obsessions, fears, addictions, and any kind of unsuitable behavior. It puts you in control of your life, your behavior, and your reactions. It strengthens your relationships, promotes patience and forbearance, and is an important tool in demonstrating you are the alpha male, and is the only tool to insure you are a fair and just pet owner.

By being aware and vigilant of your personal behavior, you will be able to be aware and vigilant of your dog's behavior. When you understand the pack mentality and give your little one confidence in your leadership they can love and respect you, and this will give you the position that you need to quickly and effectively housebreak your pet.

Chapter 2: Potty Training Basics – Getting it done in Seven Days!

Would you like to jump start the housebreaking process and have your puppy housebroken in seven days? Follow this schedule for seven straight days, and you will be well on your way to a puppy that understands exactly what is expected of him.

Adhere to 24-hour schedule. To house train your dog in 7 days, you need to meticulously follow a schedule. This will establish a routine for both you and your dog. Your puppy needs to go out first thing in the morning, after meals and play times, and before bedtime. Each moment should be accounted for. This is a sample routine for someone who is home all day.

7:00 a.m.: Time to wake up and take your puppy out to eliminate.

7:10-7:30 a.m.: Give your puppy some free time supervised by you.

7:30 a.m.: Give your puppy some food and some water.

8:00 a.m.: Take him to his designated potty spot.

8:15 a.m.: Give your puppy some free time supervised by you.

8:45 a.m.: Crate time

12:00 p.m.: Give your puppy some food and some water.

12:30 p.m.: Take him to his designated potty spot.

12:45 p.m.: Give your puppy some free time supervised by you.

1:15 p.m.: Crate time

5:00 p.m.: Give your puppy some food and some water.

5:30 p.m.: Take him to his designated potty spot.

6:15 p.m.: Crate time

8:00 p.m.: Water for an older puppy – food and water if under 4 months

8:15 p.m.: Take him to his designated potty spot.

8:30 p.m.: Give your puppy some free time supervised by you.

9:00 p.m.: Crate time

11:00 p.m.: Take him to his designated potty spot. Crate confinement overnight

During the night listen for whimpering and take your puppy outside to potty as necessary. The final chapter will cover the specifics of crate training in detail.

Like it or not, puppies need to eliminate. It can be exasperating for an owner, as puppies are not able to decipher the restrictions yet, which means elimination happens in places it should not. When puppies need to go, they go, and you must to be aware of that as an owner. This is basically the attitude that puppies take to everything, including eating, sleeping, and playing. They think of very little outside of those things. What that means is that the duty falls on you, the owner, to teach your puppy responsible behavior. You need to teach them what your requirements are, unless of course you just want them to keeping doing things the way you do not like.

Training your new puppy to potty at the right time and place can be one of the most challenging and yet important first steps for a long, happy life with each other. House soiling is a main reason dogs lose their homes or end up in shelters, as few people want to keep a dog who destroys their possessions and leaves a stinky mess to clean up.

There are three proven methods for training your puppy; frequent trips outdoors, paper training and crate training. Of course, there are positive and negative aspects of each, but they all can be prosperous if you adhere to a few basic ideas including:

- regulate your puppies diet

- have a consistent schedule for trips outside, feeding and exercise.

- provide consistent exercise

- praise your puppy for doing their business outside.

It is important to understand that the age of your puppy will determine his ability to wait to eliminate. The average measurement is one hour for each month of age. If you will pick up your puppy's water dish about two and a half hours before bedtime it will reduce the need for him to relieve himself during the night.

Chapter 3: Puppy Pads and Paper Training

In the traditional sense, paper or pad training is teaching your puppy to eliminate either on old newspapers or a pad placed in an area that is set aside as an indoor bathroom location for your puppy. Today there are options of specially made puppy pads as well as litter trays, and even fake grass boxes – but the method is still the same.

The concept is that a puppy gets used to relieving himself on paper and thus does not eliminate in places that they shouldn't. The paper absorbs and holds the urine and feces making it easier to clean up. For paper training, needed supplies include old newspapers (or pads), some food treats to reward eliminating in the right spot and some enzyme cleaning agents for the inevitable accidents. You will also possibly need an x-pen, play pen or baby gates depending on how you choose to confine your puppy to a single area when you must leave your home.

This method is one of the more difficult methods because you are offering two different options for your puppy. The ideal situation is that puppies learn to hold it indoors and only eliminate at a specific pre-ordained spot outdoors. Although this is the ideal scenario, it is not always possible due to a schedule that would make it impossible to get home several times a day. It would also be difficult for a tiny dog residing in a climate where there are brutal winters. Using the puppy pads will give your puppy the option of eliminating in an approved spot inside your home. As the dog matures, you can then work on having your dog eliminate outdoors all the time. The difficulty is that you are giving the puppy two options and at the beginning that can be just a bit confusing. But, if you stay consistent of placing the puppy regularly on the pad and giving a potty command using the same tone and same words each and every time. They will get the idea that that is the only location that is approved. But, because you will more than likely want the puppy to eliminate outdoors you will need to regularly take him out and using the same exact tone and exact same words as the indoor spot encourage him to potty in his outside designated potty spot.

This particular method relies mostly on three facts. First, puppies get accustomed to relieving themselves on the same surfaces or areas they have regularly been on previously. Secondly, puppies prefer to relieve themselves in areas where they can smell they have been before. Thirdly, puppies want to relieve themselves on softer, covered surfaces than on a cold, hard floor.

One way to do this is to paper a wide area, allow your puppy to potty there, slowly reduce the area that the papers cover then move the paper slowly to the spot you eventually want as a permanent toilet.

It is important to designate a place that is considered your puppies elimination area. Take your puppy to the same place each time. When choosing a room, opt for one with a hardwood, tiled or linoleum floor that's easily cleaned and will not soak up urine in case of accidents. It is best, if possible, to avoid carpeted areas as a puppy will prefer to relieve himself there with cushioning under his feet and not on the paper. A kitchen, bathroom or laundry room is usually ideal. An important tip would be to pick up the dirty paper as quickly as is possible. Do your best to clean it up as soon as it is dirtied. You want your puppy to be accustomed to a clean place and not even puppies want to spend time close to a large amount of their own feces and urine. However, when cleaning, keep a piece of the previously dirtied paper and use it to encourage eliminating in the spot you want. Just a small piece will be sufficient. Puppies like to eliminate where they've been previously. When they can smell a spot they've previously been, they are attracted to that spot to relieve themselves again. That is one reason why it is critical to avoid accidents, and why a thorough cleaning is necessary when there are accidents to avoid your puppy repeating that behavior.

Here are some techniques for proper cleanup for puppy accidents. With new accidents, pick up the solids and blot up as much liquid as possible. Do not use using ammonia-based cleaning products. Because urine has ammonia in it, those products may imitate the smell and make the area even more desirable as a spot for elimination. Once urine has dried on carpets or even walls it is even more difficult to discover exactly where the urine is located. If you will invest in a high quality black light you will be able to discover each and every accident site as the light will cause the urine to glow in the dark. Remember to check vertical areas such as walls and bedspreads that leg-lifting dogs like to target. To successfully clean urine you will not want a product that only covers up the area with perfumes, but one that will neutralize the foul-smelling urine. Urine is made of stick urea, urochrome (yellow color) and uric acid. The first two can be washed away, but uric acid is extremely difficult to break up and to remove from the surface. Successful products will not only clean away the urea and urochrome, but they will also neutralize the uric acid with enzymes or encapsulate the urine molecules that will contain the odor.

With paper training, you can use this in your favor by keeping some old soiled paper, and placing it in the area you would like your puppy to eliminate. It is best to put the designated potty area away from their bed and water. Carefully watch your puppy and if they try to eliminate in an area not covered by paper intercept and redirect them to the paper. Praise them when they successfully use the paper.

Any time they do eliminate on the paper by themselves, you also want to praise them heavily and offer some type of treat. This will help to more quickly encourage relieving themselves on the paper.

It is critical to make a schedule if you wish to have successfully housebreak your puppy. Your puppy has a tiny little bladder and liquid runs right through them. This is also true for food, it goes in and pretty much comes back out. It is very important to make sure you give your puppy many opportunities to eliminate outside and do the right thing. It is also helpful to know as it won't be very long at all after eating or drinking that you will need to take your puppy to his designated area. Ten to twenty minutes after eating your puppy will be needed to be taken out.

As mentioned before, a good standard is that dogs can control their bladders for the number of hours corresponding to their age in months up to about nine months to a year. Be aware that that ten to twelve hours is a long time for anyone to hold it! A six-month-old puppy can rationally be required to hold it for about six hours. However, each puppy is an individual and the time factor will be different for each one. Size of the dog will also play a factor in how long they can hold it.

With very young puppies, you should expect to take the puppy out the very first thing in the morning and the very last thing at night. Just like a human baby, you will have to listen for whimpering and take your puppy to empty his bladder a few times a night especially if your puppy is under four months. He will need an opportunity to eliminate after playing, after waking from a nap, after chewing and playing with his toys, after eating and after drinking. In those very early days you could be taking your puppy out to his designated potty area a dozen times or more in a twenty-four-hour period. But, that diligence will pay off in huge dividends as your puppy will learn much more effectively and quickly what is expected of him regarding proper elimination. There are challenges that may have to be navigated. If you work you may need to make arrangements, be it taking your dog to work, hiring a dog walker, or enlisting the help of a friend or family member to ensure that early schedule is consistently adhered to. The sooner you convey the idea that there is an approved place to potty and places that are off limits, the more quickly you'll be able to put this messy chapter of your life behind you.

It is imperative to carefully evaluate your puppy and to discover his individual signals and indicators for the need to eliminate. Some puppies may be able to wait longer than others. Some puppies will have to go out each time they get excited or play hard. Some will lose control of their bladder if their owner expresses anger to them. Canine potty habits are certainly idiosyncratic, but all puppies, if evaluated, will give signals to express their intentions. Some signals might include whining, squatting, walking in circles, or sniffing around. When your very young puppy give you his indicator, pick him up right then and carry him to his designated potty spot. Do not expect him to walk to his potty spot, as he may not be able to make it.

Before deciding upon this method to housebreak your pet, we need to evaluate some of the disadvantages of this method in order for you to make a truly informed decision.

The main disadvantage of this technique is that you are training your puppy that it is okay to relieve himself inside your home. Now, if you plan to have a permanent indoor potty spot for your dog this is okay, but if your plans are to eventually have them relieve themselves outside this method as mentioned before can be confusing to your puppy. Because of this confusion, housebreaking generally takes a bit longer with this method and there are generally more accidents as well.

A second disadvantage of this method is that any papers accidently left lying around can be a target for elimination on by your puppy. If a newspaper is inadvertently left on the floor you may find some bad news inside!

A third disadvantage is that you will have more clean-up as the papers will need to be removed as quickly as possible for health and hygiene reasons. This method has the potential to leave your home smelling more like a kennel than a family dwelling.

A forth disadvantage is that some pets trained in this manner will use only paper and that will make training them to use the designated spot outside substantially more difficult.

This method of training is much more easily done in a practical sense with small dogs due to the sheer volume of waste that can be produced by a larger breed.

Chapter 4: The Diet of Your Puppy

Another extremely important factor is to control the diet. The digestive systems of puppies are immature and they are not able to handle a lot of food at one time. It is recommended that you break up the feedings into three or four small meals. Another very important factor is to give your puppy a high-quality food that is designed for puppies and has the greatest nutritional value and one that agrees with your puppy's digestion system.

Being aware of your puppy's stool is a very good way to determine if his diet is agreeable or not. If you are seeing consistent stools that are bulky, stinky or loose, you may want to discuss alternative food options with your vet. When a puppy is over-fed, it can cause diarrhea and that makes housetraining even more challenging. Also, especially during that very important first year, do not feed your puppy human food. It is truly best for your dog if human food is never a part of his diet.

One of the dangers of overfeeding is food bloat. Some breeds are more susceptible than others, but each owner needs to be aware. Puppies may be too young to figure out when their little tummies are full or may gobble their food too quickly. They may continue eating, or snacking, when they are not even hungry. Eating too much can cause food bloat. Over-eating can even cause a life-threatening condition called gastric dilation-volvulus. GDV simply means your puppy is in danger of suffering from a twisted stomach from overeating. The belly becomes distended and there can be unsuccessful retching and excessive salivating. It would be important to call your vet if you notice these symptoms as they can be life threatening.

Another danger of over-eating could be obesity. Your puppy is not able to understand how much food he needs, many times if there is food available he will eat it resulting in obesity. You do not want a chubby puppy that turns into a chubby adult dog as the negative health effects will shorten your dog's lifespan and possibly incur unwanted vet bills. The same maladies that plague overweight humans (diabetes, heart problems and hypothyroidism) tend to also plague overweight dogs. Healthy eating habits as a puppy usually translate to healthy habits in the adult dog.

A good diet will also help prevent skeletal problems. Puppy food is filled with a high amount of nutrients and the proper calories needed to build strong bones and teeth. Puppy formula will help your baby grow into a healthy adult. Too much food will accelerate his growth too quickly causing his little body to go into overdrive and create bone too quickly. A result would be the possibility of skeletal and joint problems as he ages. Some large breeds are especially susceptible. Similar problems can result from feeding puppy food to your adult dog.

We want to get it just right and since a puppy's eyes are bigger than his stomach he may feel he needs more food than he does. Because of his stomach being so small, he will need to eat many small meals as opposed to one or two big ones. Four meals a day until around four months old is a good rule of thumb. Then you can try lowering it to three slightly larger meals. By around six months of age you should be able to feed him twice daily. Study your breed to know the benefits and pitfalls. If you have a mixed breed then concentrate on his dominate breed and do your best to accommodate his needs. Some smaller breeds will mature faster some as early as ten months of age. While other larger breeds may take up to a couple of years to mature. Your vet is a good place to gather the needed information for your particular dog breed.

Another thing to be work on with your puppy is the fact you do not want him aggressive over his food. From the time he is very small, periodically take away his food as he begins eating and return it shortly after. Another thing to do is to place your hand into his dish while he is eating and take food out or move his food around with your hand. Your puppy needs to understand that you have full authority of his food area. Puppies that are allowed to eat without any distractions or challenges can become very aggressive and attack anyone who dares to enter the sacred area of their food bowl. To prevent this from happening make sure that you do this often during the first six months and periodically afterwards as a refresher course. The same is true with rawhides and such, your puppy needs to know that you can take away his food and toys anytime you please. Since you give it back shortly he will begin to understand he will not go hungry, and these actions will give you freedom to be in his food area. If possible when he is young have people that are not in your household to do the same procedures with him. It could save an attack over him protecting his food bowl in the future.

Chapter 5: The Importance of Praise

The importance of praising your puppy cannot be over emphasized. There are times when a puppy will need to be scolded or corrected; but if you scold or punish a puppy after he has soiled your rug or floor he will not understand what you are doing and it will only confuse and alienate him. And to be honest, that soiling was your fault. You did not watch for his indicators that he was in need to go out and potty. You will need both positive and negative reinforcements to train your puppy, but you must be fair and just with your puppy. You wouldn't spank a baby for pooping in his diaper and neither is it just to discipline a puppy who is still trying to figure out this business of where and when he can and can't go potty. Go over the top with praise and excitement when your puppy goes outside. Give a little treat, cheer, clap, cuddle whatever it takes to let that little one to understand that he did great! Be effusive in letting him know that nothing is more important than him going potty in his designated place!

It is wise to keep your puppy in a contained area that has no rugs if possible during the training process. If you missed the cues, or no one was available to take him out – just clean it up and promise yourself that YOU will do better next time. It would be wise to invest in a cleaner that will kill odors and help remove the scent so he is not tempted by the smell to use that spot again. It is vital that you read labels very carefully and make sure that the cleaner is not toxic to your little one! If your puppy urinates on your carpet, blot of as much of the liquid as is possible before applying cleaners.

Since prevention is the key thing, if you catch the dog starting to squat pick him up and rush outside. If he does his business then praise, praise, praise! If you are trying to show him the pad is his alternative indoor spot you could carry him there.

When it comes to housetraining, prevention is the key factor that will enable you to be quickly successful in this endeavor.

A dog's size is also going to be a factor in potty training. "Toy" dogs can be trained with diligence, but it will take a great deal of consistency and perhaps a bit more time. If your little dog is going to spend many hours without the opportunity to eliminate some trainers recommend teaching little dogs to use potty boxes designed for indoor use or even the puppy pads. This is a concept much like a kitty litter box for cats.

If your puppy keeps eliminating indoors in the same spot where he has had an accident it is probably because you didn't clean up the urine effectively and there is residual odor remaining.

A common mistake is giving your dog the run of the house before they are truly ready. A pet owner feels like their puppy has the idea or has behaved well and declare victory too soon. Then they are angry when they come to a destroyed piece of furniture or mess on the floor. There are times when the owner is away and either the puppy gets excited, fearful or most common just plain ole bored. The pet owner comes back to a mess and the puppy has no understanding of why he is in so much trouble and why his owner is angry with him.

Chapter 6: Understanding a Urinary Tract Infection

If your puppy has gone an extensive time with success and then out of the blue begins to urinate indoors one of the first things to do is to make sure that are no physical issues promoting this behavior. A urinary tract infection or bladder infection can many times cause your pet to have issues with elimination.

Here are some tips to determine if your puppy or dog has a urinary tract infection and what to do about it. If you puppy is needing more trips outside it is because a urinary tract infection gives an increased urge to urinate usually resulting in more whining, barking and trips to the yard. You may also find yourself needing to refill their water bowl more often, as dogs with UTIs are generally thirstier – this also accounts for the increase in urination. Sometimes a dog with a UTI will need to go so often they stop trying to go to their designated outside location, or pad. Because the urge to urinate is sudden and uncontrollable it will result in a regression in this area of potty training. Another symptom of a serious UTI would be blood. Blood in your dog's urine is never a good sign, and this symptom can be especially tricky to detect – unless, of course, the urine is on your favorite white carpet. Blood oftentimes looks brown and not red, so be aware. A round of antibiotics from your vet can have your puppy feeling better in just a few days.

Chapter 7: Training Without a Crate and Without Puppy Pads

There are people who just do not like the idea of putting their puppy in a crate, or even have adopted a puppy that was abused and a crate was involved, or even the fact that they may just not have room for a crate. Regardless of the reason, the good news is that you can succeed at house training without a crate if you can devote 100% of your time to this endeavor.

The only way to successfully housebreak your puppy is to give the puppy constant supervision. This particular method is best suited to people who can spend all day with their puppy. People that work from home, or the retired. It's also a preferred method for people who just do not agree with the use of a crate, or have a crate phobic puppy or dog.

What Is 'Constant Supervision' House Training?

We will cover a range of procedures that do not involve the use of a crate. This method will rely on constantly watching your dog or puppy.

Using a crate takes of advantage of the fact a puppy will not potty inside their den if it isn't roomy enough that they can toilet at one end and sleep at the other. In crate method an unsupervised puppy is placed into a crate. However, if you are not using a crate, no other confined space will be small enough that your puppy is deterred from eliminating in there.

If you choose to train your puppy without a crate you have no opportunity to take your eyes off of your puppy and still be guaranteed that they won't soil your carpet. Each mistake is a missed teaching time to train to do the right thing. This results in a backward step in training as well as cleaning up the mess that your puppy made.

So, the only fast tract to success is constant, and this does mean constant, supervision. You must be diligent to watch him to make sure he does not eliminate on your floors and carpet; which means he cannot be left unsupervised.

Therefore, the only quick path to success is constant, and I mean CONSTANT supervision. You must watch them like a hawk to be sure he won't potty on your floors and carpets. He can never be left unsupervised.

This method means a puppy that is not housebroken can never be left alone or unwatched in the home. A puppy can relieve himself where he shouldn't in a matter of a few seconds, and to train your puppy properly this must be prevented. You will need to be aware of your puppies indicators that he is about to relieve himself and be ready to take them to their designated potty location. Each puppy will have their own unique indicator, but generally it will be sniffing the ground, whining, attempting to get to a quiet location, circling or even squatting. The pet owner will need to be aware of their puppies behavior at all times to prevent accidents or immediately correct them by getting them immediately to the proper spot with a firm "No!" for the action.

You may be thinking that this sounds like a LOT of work and truly it is, but there are ways to make this training method a bit easier.

Most often when a puppy is sitting in your lap or sleeping near you they will not eliminate on you, so that would give an opportunity for a bit of relaxation of your guard. When you are going to be in different rooms you could attach them to the leash and keep them with you, which will help you realize when they need to go and also prevent them from sneaking off to relieve themselves. In this method of training it is imperative that you either are watching them or that there is a physical connection to know exactly what they are doing at all times.

Also, the use of this method of training requires extreme diligence; it is the method that requires the least equipment. With this method, you will not need puppy pads, crates or play pens. You will need a collar, leash, food treats and enzyme cleaners for the occasional accident. It is unreasonable to assume that during this training time you will never leave your puppy, so you may need a sectioned off area (preferable puppy proofed), use a baby gate or some type of way to contain your puppy when you do have to leave, along with pads for the inevitable accident. It would be wise to have a location that is easily cleaned.

Ways to create a sanctioned area would be to use a baby gate or pet barrier to limit your puppy to a single room, usually one with no carpet. You can also purchase a puppy "x-pen" which effectively fences off a small section to keep your puppy contained to that particular location. These spaces must be large enough for bedding, water at one end and newspaper or puppy pads at the other.

To be fair, training without a crate is the most difficult method as trying to constantly supervise anything is challenging. Even those who work from home or are retired have cooking, cleaning, laundry, calls, chores and more. By comparison, accidents will be more likely without a temporarily space to confine your puppy during the time they are supposed to be holding their bladder. Since you are not giving an alternative indoor potty area such in paper or pad training, you will always have to be on high alert for those indicators that your puppy needs to go. If you have the time and are always home, this method is effective and you are sure to succeed.

Regardless of the method of choice for you, any puppy needs to be closely supervised and interrupted when they are ready to eliminate in a spot that is not their designated potty area.

Chapter 8: Crate Training

Crate training is the most effective, fool proof and humane method to train your puppy, especially if your goal is to train your puppy in seven days! Some believe crate training a dog to be cruel or barbaric. However, if you will evaluate crate training from a dog's viewpoint, you will find that it actually meets an innate desire for a safe place to call his own. Dogs are basically what we call den animals. It is in their genetic makeup to want a secure and sheltered area to rest. Many times in the effort to create their own "den" a puppy or dog will curl up in a box or under a low table. Crate training can help to satisfy this very natural instinct in your puppy, and will provide you with several benefits as well. Offering your dog its own crate meets your pet's instinctive needs and allows you some control in housebreaking endeavors.

So understanding what makes a good crate for your puppy would be your first step. The most effective crate is one that is just barely big enough so that your dog can lie, stand and turn around. If you give the puppy too much space it will destroy the den concept, and will give your pet the option of soiling half of the crate and still having a clean area in which to rest.

There are a variety of materials and brands to choose from. The next decision will be whether plastic or wire will work best for your puppy's needs. Crates that are made from molded plastic are easy to clean, draft-free and because of the limited visibility are more like dens. Depending on your dogs size and type of coat and what conveniences you will need in a crate, plastic may be what you are looking to use. Some advantages to a plastic crate are that they provide better insulation for your puppy.

If you own a puppy, small dog, or dog with a short coat, then plastic crates can help him to retain more of his body heat. This can be helpful in cold or wet climates. This may be a disadvantage if you live in a warmer climate or have a long haired dog. Another benefit to a plastic crate is the fact that it offers more privacy. With generally fewer openings for the dog to see out it will give a feeling of a safe den-like space. The fact that the puppy's view is blocked will eliminate some things that might distract him and cause him to whine and cry. If travel is in your foreseeable future, a plastic crate can be airline approved, whereas a wire crate cannot. If travel is in the foreseeable future for you and your puppy, first check with your airlines to make sure the plastic dog crate of your choice would meet their safety guidelines. There are several types of plastic dog crates that come apart for storage. Some crates are designed for the top to be removable so that the bottom can be used as a dog bed. Not every crate has these versatile features, so read carefully what your crate is capable of doing before purchasing. Generally, even a bigger plastic dog crate can be very light, which is something to consider if you will be moving the crate often.

Although there are many positive features, the plastic crate does have downsides. In a plastic crate there is a decreased amount of ventilation and air movement. So the crate has to potential to become very stuffy for your pet. Another disadvantage is that your pet may feel too isolated. If your puppy is very people oriented or has become very attached to you, the plastic crate may make him feel isolated and separated from you. Storage can take more room as a plastic crate cannot fold flat and will not breakdown to the degree that a wire or soft sided type will. The biggest disadvantage to a plastic crate is that plastic is porous and the odors can become imbedded in the material of the crate itself. This makes it more difficult to keep the crate clean.

Many dog owners prefer a wire dog crate as they have the great advantage of providing excellent ventilation. Because of their wire mesh panels they are also the best selection for dogs that have chewing habits since it is impossible for them to chew through stainless steel or galvanized wire. Another advantage of wire crates is they are completely collapsible which enables easy storage and ease when they must be transported from one location to another. A number of brands come with a divider panel; this will be extremely helpful as your puppy increases size. Some brands feature a two door system with one door on the front and one door on the backside of the crate. In these particular crates the doors are usually secured by wire mesh hooks or by a drop pin. Wire crates are generally made from powder coated or galvanized steel or stainless steel. One of the main highlights in the "pro" category for the wire crate is that there is normally a plastic pan at the bottom which will slide in and out for easy cleaning. The excellent ventilation also makes for a reduction of trapped odors.

Wire dog crates come in a variety of sizes and most offer divider panels. If getting a large breed puppy, you can buy a larger crate than he's needs so he can still use it when he reaches his adult size. Considering a crate can be one of the more expensive items you'll buy for your dog, this can save you money in the long run. A divider can be used to keep two dogs separated without getting a second kennel, or can be helpful if you have a puppy that will grow to be a large size dog. It will save you money by only having to buy one crate that will last your puppies growing spurt. When a small puppy is in a large crate the "den like" experience is lost, a divider wall can give that secure closed in feeling. This problem is overcome with a divider panel that can be adjusted as your puppy grows.

Your puppy may grow to enjoy the run of the house, but sometimes he needs to be put in his crate. A wire general cage dog crate allows your dog to feel more like a part of what is going on in your home because he can see what is going on around him. Wire crates provide a better view if car traveling is something that is frequently done.

Nothing is perfect and a wire crate is not an exception. A disadvantage is that even when there are perfectly assembled they can have a loose feel about them. In time the doors can lose their alignment making the locking feature harder to use. Also a very large wire crate can be bulky and heavy making it awkward or difficult to move. Because a wire crate offers great ventilation it may need to be covered to keep out drafts and to make it appear more den-like.

Once a crate has been purchased, you will want to give your puppy or dog time to investigate. Just leave the crate on the floor with the door open until your puppy becomes used to having it around. Placing dog treats and a towel might help your puppy gain an interest in exploring the crate. After your puppy is familiar with the crate, close your dog inside the crate for ten to fifteen minutes. Stay right there with your puppy perhaps even putting your fingers through the wire of the crate. Your puppy needs to be assured that this new environment is safe and secure. After ten or fifteen minutes open the door and let the puppy stay or leave at his will. This should be done several times that first day getting your little one accustomed to his crate. The crate is to be his safe space and should never be used to punish your puppy. The time in the crate should be as enjoyable as is possible. Toys and treats can help to establish this setting of harmony and peace.

Crate training helps you teach your little one not to use the bathroom inside. Dogs instinctively desire to keep their den clean. Dogs do not want to sleep in a soiled area and will do all within their power to hold it until they are taken to their designated potty spot. If you have a crate that is the proper fit for your puppy he is going to do all in his power to refrain from using the bathroom until you let him outside. Crate training makes it a simple way to schedule regular trips to his designated potty spot.

It is important to determine the crate's ideal location. You need to put the crate in a location that will remain consistent. This may be a high-traffic area where your family spends a lot of time, but you may also want to provide the dog with some rest time removed from activity, especially at night. Dogs are social animals and some breed even more so than others. They enjoy being near their family so that they can see what is going on around them and can feel like a part of things. This is very fulfilling to a dog. Since being in a crate should be a positive experience and they should want to spend time there, you don't want to stick them away in a quiet room or out of the way place in the house. They will feel punished, excluded and isolated; and that will not make for a serine, happy puppy. Make sure you place the crate in a busy area of the home where they are able to see and hear what is going on with their family. Usually kitchen or living room areas are ideal locations for a crate. Keep in mind that you would like this area to be free of uncomfortable drafts, not too close to a heat source (radiator, fireplace or vent). You will want to avoid direct sunlight. As much as you are able to give the location of your crate should be neither too hot nor too cold.

If your puppy is very young, you may want to consider moving the crate into your bedroom at night, or placing them in a portable carrier or second crate. The very young puppy has just gone from being with his mother and perhaps siblings to being alone. This can leave them stressed and feeling abandoned which will result in whining and crying. You don't want to make the mistake of putting the puppy in bed with you as that will confuse him as to who is the alpha – him or you. But, neither do you want him to feel frightened and alone.

A puppy will get great comfort and a feeling of safety and security being able to sleep near their family, especially during those first few days in a strange new place.

It isn't essential you have them sleep in your bedroom with you, but it may be beneficial. After a few days, begin to move the crate slowly to where you want them to sleep as they have time to adjust to their new environment. Simply move the crate further away every few nights until you have removed them from the bedroom and where you want them to be.

Some ideas of the proper toys and bedding to place in your crate would be tough chew toys. There are many benefits to leaving two or three tough chew toys in the crate with your puppy. It will provide your puppy with something to occupy their minds and keep them from becoming bored. It will give them an alternative to chewing up their bedding, which could be detrimental to their health. It reinforces that being in the crate is a time for some of their favorite things, thus making the crate a happy place for them. It also will help reduce the likelihood of your puppy chewing on your belongings.

It is important to be aware that soft stuffed teddy bears and easily chewed squeaky toys should only be given to your puppy under supervision and never left in the crate. They will likely get destroyed, but your puppy could inject pieces causing intestinal blockages.

The most important thing about crate training is to follow a strict schedule so that your puppy becomes accustomed to routine! If this sample schedule is adhered to you will be well on your way to having your puppy potty trained in record time!

Adhere to a 24-hour schedule. To house train your dog in 7 days, you need to meticulously follow a schedule. This will establish a routine for both you and your dog. Your puppy needs to go out first thing in the morning, after meals and play times, and before bedtime. Each moment should be accounted for. This is a sample routine for someone who is home all day.

7:00 a.m.: Time to wake up and take your puppy out to eliminate.

7:10-7:30 a.m.: Give your puppy some free time supervised by you.

7:30 a.m.: Give your puppy some food and some water.

8:00 a.m.: Take him to his designated potty spot.

8:15 a.m.: Give your puppy some free time supervised by you.

8:45 a.m.: Crate time

12:00 p.m.: Give your puppy some food and some water.

12:30 p.m.: Take him to his designated potty spot.

12:45 p.m.: Give your puppy some free time supervised by you.

1:15 p.m.: Crate time

5:00 p.m.: Give your puppy some food and some water.

5:30 p.m.: Take him to his designated potty spot.

6:15 p.m.: Crate time

8:00 p.m.: Water for an older puppy – food and water if under 4 months

8:15 p.m.: Take him to his designated potty spot.

8:30 p.m.: Give your puppy some free time supervised by you.

9:00 p.m.: Crate time

11:00 p.m.: Take him to his designated potty spot. Crate confinement overnight

Make sure to give your puppy a bathroom break during the night. The maximum time you are able to leave a young puppy is four hours so with a very young puppy you will need to set your alarm clock for every two to three hours. After the alarm goes off take your puppy out of the crate and give him a chance to relieve himself in his designated potty spot. Then quietly put him back into the crate. Older dogs can wait longer, but you need to make sure they do not go in their crate overnight, or all that hard work in the day time is basically undone. During this time do not fuss or even speak to the puppy except to give him his potty instructions – the same words and same tone as during the day. You don't want to give him the idea that night-time is play time.

A crate is an ideal place to keep your belongings safe and secure and your puppy safe and secure while you are away. Another thought is that a crate is also the most secure and convenient way to transport your dog as it will keep him protected while in the car and is a necessity for airline travel.

As with anything, a crate can be abused. You may be tempted to keep your puppy there throughout the day or to use it as a way to punish him. This will just undermine the training process and perhaps make your puppy hate the crate when it should in fact be his haven!

When you are crate training all feedings initially should be done inside of the crate. Make sure you leave the door open while you are feeding your puppy. The association with food will make it a great place for him.

Your puppy needs you as the owner to be consistent in your routine but also in the words you use to instruct him. Just as you will want to use the same phrase with the same exact inflection when teaching your puppy his designated potty spot; you will also want to use the same phrase and same inflection when instructing him to get inside of his crate. You need to choose the same word each time. A command such as "crate time" or "get in your Kennel" with the same exact hand gesture will help him to understand what is expected of him. When the puppy goes in say the command, and when you feed him at meal times say the same command. When your puppy obeys give him a treat to show him your pleasure. It is best that your puppy not associate his crate with being alone. So in the early days of training make sure that you or someone familiar is able to be with him as he acclimates to his crate. Those early days can also be benefited by keeping a puppy journal. It may sound impractical to keep a journal of the times your puppy needs to go potty, but it may in fact prevent unwanted accidents to have a written documentation of his successes and his accidents. A regular feeding schedule will help to insure a more regular bathroom schedule. Remember it is critical to not punish your puppy for accidents, teaching your puppy to eliminate outdoors is a process that takes patience and time.

Chapter 9: Conclusion

Being a pet owner is one of the most fulfilling roles available to mankind. The love and adoration so freely given can be so gratifying. The soothing sensation of running your hands down their fur and looking into deep loving eyes can make the coldest heart melt. That exuberance and devotion that is lavished completely on you just for showing up can make your feel like a million dollars! If you want to be needed and to be loved, a dog is usually hands down the best choice of all.

However, with that love, acceptance and devotions comes responsibility and commitment! I think we have all seen the videos and clips of dogs with their bones showing through their skin, whimpering in the cold; unloved, uncared for and neglected. We all wonder to ourselves – how could anyone do something so dastardly? I can't imagine anyone starting out to neglect and harm their pet, but yet we have seen that scenario take place. Dog ownership is not something to be entered into frivolously. Owning a dog is a long-term emotional and financial obligation. Before deciding that a certain dog is right for you, you must make an honest assessment as to whether your home is right for any dog.

Before getting a puppy you need to ask yourself a few questions:

- Do I have the finances to own a dog?
- Is my space adequate for a dog?
- Is my schedule adaptable to having a dog?
- Am I willing to commit to training my dog?
- Can I control my emotions when angry or frustrated?

If you answered yes to the above questions, then you are ready to enjoy the pleasures and enjoyment of being a dog owner! You and your family members should decide who will be responsible for food, water, walking, exercise, clean-up and grooming. Post a schedule of tasks in a visible area of the house to remind everyone of their responsibilities.

It is always a wise idea to Dog-Proof Your Home! Prepare your home before your new dog arrives. Move breakables or "chewables" to higher ground. Make electrical cords inaccessible to inquisitive paws and noses. Block off any area of the house that you want off-limits. Put the lid down on your toilet and your shoes up in your closet. Block off access or put away plants that may be toxic to dogs.

And last but not least, enjoy your new puppy and make many happy memories that you will cherish for a lifetime!

Made in the USA
Lexington, KY
04 October 2017